teacher's friend publications

Winter

a creative idea book
for the
elementary teacher

written and illustrated
by
Karen Sevaly

poems by
Margaret Bolz

Copyright © 1990
Teacher's Friend Publications, Inc.
All rights reserved.
Printed in the United States of America.
Published by Teacher's Friend Publications, Inc.
7407 Orangewood Drive, Riverside, CA 92504

ISBN 0-943263-15-8

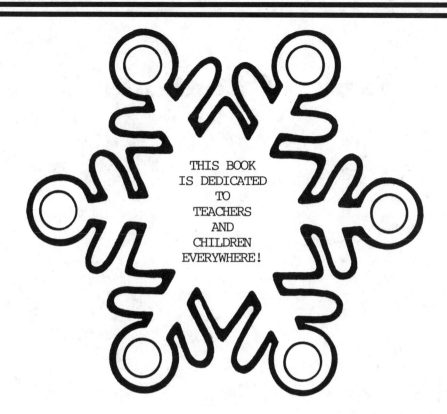

THIS BOOK
IS DEDICATED
TO
TEACHERS
AND
CHILDREN
EVERYWHERE!

Table of Contents

Notes

Let's Make It!

Children are especially responsive to the various holidays and themes associated with the four seasons. Teacher's Friend has published the "Winter" Idea Book, to assist teachers in motivating students, with this in mind.

WHO USES THIS BOOK:

Preschool and elementary teachers along with Scout leaders, Sunday School teachers and parents all love the monthly and seasonal idea books.

Each idea or craft can easily be adapted to fit a wide range of grade levels. Kindergarteners can color and cut out the simple, bold patterns while older students love expanding these same patterns and crafts to a more complex format. Most of the ideas and activities are open-ended. Teachers may add their own curriculum appropriate for the grade level they teach. Young children may practice number, color or letter recognition while older students may like to drill multiplication facts or match homonyms.

WHAT YOU'LL FIND IN THIS BOOK:

Teachers and parents will find a variety of crafts, activities, bulletin board ideas and patterns that compliment the monthly holidays and seasonal themes. Children will be delighted with the booklet covers, bingo cards, name tags, mobiles, place cards, writing pages and gameboards. There is also a special section devoted to the sport of the season!

HOW TO USE THIS BOOK:

Every page of this book may be duplicated for individual classroom use. Some pages are meant to be used as duplicating masters or student worksheets. Most of the crafts and patterns may be copied onto construction paper or printed on index paper. Children can then make the crafts by cutting them out and coloring them with crayons or colored markers.

Many of the pages can be enlarged with an overhead or opaque projector. The patterns can then be used for door displays, bulletin boards or murals.

MOBILES:

Making mobiles are especially fun for all ages. Teachers may like to simplify mobile construction for younger children by using one of these ideas.

DRINKING STRAW MOBILE - Thread a piece of yarn through a plastic drinking straw and tie a mobile pattern to each end. Flatten a paper clip and bend it around the center of the straw for hanging. The mobile can easily be balanced by adjusting the yarn. (Older students can make their mobiles the same way but may wish to add additional levels by hanging other mobiles directly below the first.)

CLOTHES HANGER MOBILE - Mobiles can easily be made with a wire clothes hanger, as shown. Just tie each pattern piece to the hanger with thread, yarn or kite string.

YARN MOBILE - The most simple mobile is made by gluing the pattern pieces to a length of yarn, each piece spaced directly beneath the other. Tie a bow at the top and hang in a window or from the ceiling.

CLIP ART PAGES:

The illustrations on these pages may be used in classroom bulletins, newspapers, notes home or just to decorate your own worksheets. Cut the illustrations out and paste them to your originals before printing. The drawings may be enlarged or reduced on some copy machines. You are also free to enlarge the characters for other uses, such as; bulletin boards, calendar decorations, booklet covers and awards.

PLACE CARDS OR NAME TAGS:

If possible, laminate the finished name tags or place cards. Use a special dry transfer marker or dark crayon to write the names on the laminated surface. After the special day, simply wipe off the letters with a tissue for use at another time.

POETRY:

Children love clever poems. Use the poems in this book to inspire your students and at the same time record the improvement in their handwriting.

Each morning, copy one or two lines, or an entire poem, on the class chalkboard. Ask the children to copy it in their best handwriting. Have them write the date at the top of the page. The children can then collect the poems chronologically in a notebook. This is a great way to show parents how their child's handwriting has improved.

STAND-UP CHARACTERS:

All of the stand-up characters in this book can easily be made from construction or index paper. Children can add the color and cut them out. The characters can be used as table decorations, name cards or used in a puppet show.

The characters can also be enlarged on posterboard for a bulletin board display or reduced in size for use in a diorama or as finger puppets.

BULLETIN BOARDS:

Creating clever bulletin boards can be a fun experience for you and your students. Many of the bulletin board ideas in this book contain patterns that the students can make themselves. You simply need to cover the board with bright paper, (preferably only once a year) and display the appropriate heading. Students make their own pumpkins for a classroom pumpkin patch or creative writing apples for a Johnny Appleseed display.

Many of the illustrations in this book can also be enlarged and displayed on a bulletin board. Use an over-head or opaque projector to do your enlargements. When you enlarge a character, think BIG! Figures three, four or even five feet tall can make a dramatic display. Use colored butcher paper for large displays eliminating the need to add color with markers or crayons.

WHATEVER YOU DO....

Have fun using the ideas in this book. Be creative! Develop your own ideas and adapt the patterns and crafts to fit your own curriculum. By using your imagination, you will be encouraging your students to be more creative. A creative classroom is a fun classroom! One that promotes an enthusiasm for learning!

WINTER

WINTER ACTIVITIES

SNOWMAN SEQUENCE CARDS

WINTER BULLETIN BOARDS

MR. SNOWMAN

JACK FROST

WINTER MOBILE

CREATIVE WRITING MITTENS

Winter Activities

CATCH A SNOWFLAKE

The next time it snows, have your students run outside and catch snowflakes on pieces of dark colored construction paper. Ask them to examine the snowflakes carefully and see if there are any two snowflakes alike. (For best results, keep the construction paper in a refrigerator so that the snowflakes melt more slowly.)

WINTER IMPROVISATIONS

Ask your students to act out the life of a snowflake. The children will love pantomining the forming of the snowflake, floating to the ground and eventually melting.

FREEZING WATERS

Winter is a great time of year to teach children what happens to water when it freezes!

Cut the top off a large tin can and fill it completely with water. Place the can in the freezer or outside overnight, if your weather is cold enough. The next morning, ask students to examine the level of the water.

Older children may like to research the reasons why some substances contract while others expand when frozen.

This would be a great time to make frozen popsicles that the whole class can enjoy!

Winter Activities

ABOUT THE SEASONS

What is the real reason
That we have each season?

When it's WINTER and it rains and snows,
We bundle up like Eskimos.

Flowers and blossoms cover the ground
When winter is finished and SPRING comes around.

We readily know it's SUMMER we've got
When the temperature's high and the sun is hot.

Then AUTUMN comes when the weather is chilly,
When cold crisp winds blow willy-nilly.

There are these seasons, numbering four.
When all are finished, they repeat once more.

Winter Bingo

This game offers an exciting way to introduce students to the winter season. Give each child a copy of the bingo words listed below or write the words on the chalkboard. Ask students to write any 24 words on his or her bingo card. Use the same directions you might use for regular bingo.

WINTER	SLED	STOCKINGS	SHADOW
COLD	SKIS	REINDEER	LINCOLN
FREEZE	SLOPES	HANUKKAH	WASHINGTON
SNOW	DECEMBER	CANDLES	VALENTINE
ICE	JANUARY	NEW YEAR	HEARTS
ICICLE	FEBRUARY	MIDNIGHT	CUPID
MITTENS	CHRISTMAS	RESOLUTION	LOVE
JACKET	HOLIDAY	CELEBRATE	FLOWERS
SNOWFLAKE	GIFTS	MARTIN LUTHER KING	CANDY
SNOWMAN	SANTA	GROUNDHOG	LEAP YEAR

WINTER BINGO

FREE

WINTER NEWS

A NOTE HOME TO PARENTS

_____

_____

_____

_____

_____

_____

_____

_____

_____

_____

_____

_____

_____

_____

_____

_____

_____

_____

_____

_____

_____

_____

_____

_____

_____

Snowman Sequence Cards

Winter Bulletin Boards

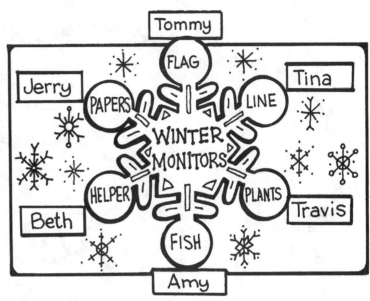

WINTER MONITORS

Liven up that old monitor bulletin board with a new winter theme. Display a large snowflake in the middle of the board and label each branch of the snowflake with a job to be done. Children's names can be written on smaller snowflakes, or strips of paper, and placed next to each job. Rotate the names during the winter months. This idea can also be used for reading or math groups.

CHILLY REPORTS

Display a winter weather character off to the side of the class bulletin board. Students can write reports about their winter weather observations. The reports can be shown on the board with paper icicles hanging from each one. The title "Chilling Reports" can be cut from white styrofoam trays for a 3-D effect.

CLASSY SNOWPEOPLE

Children will love making and then displaying look-a-like snowpeople. Have each student cut out a large white paper snowman. Ask them to draw in the features to resemble themselves. They may like to add items which depict their interests. Line the snowpeople up along a class bulletin board and ask students to guess who's who.

Winter Weather Character

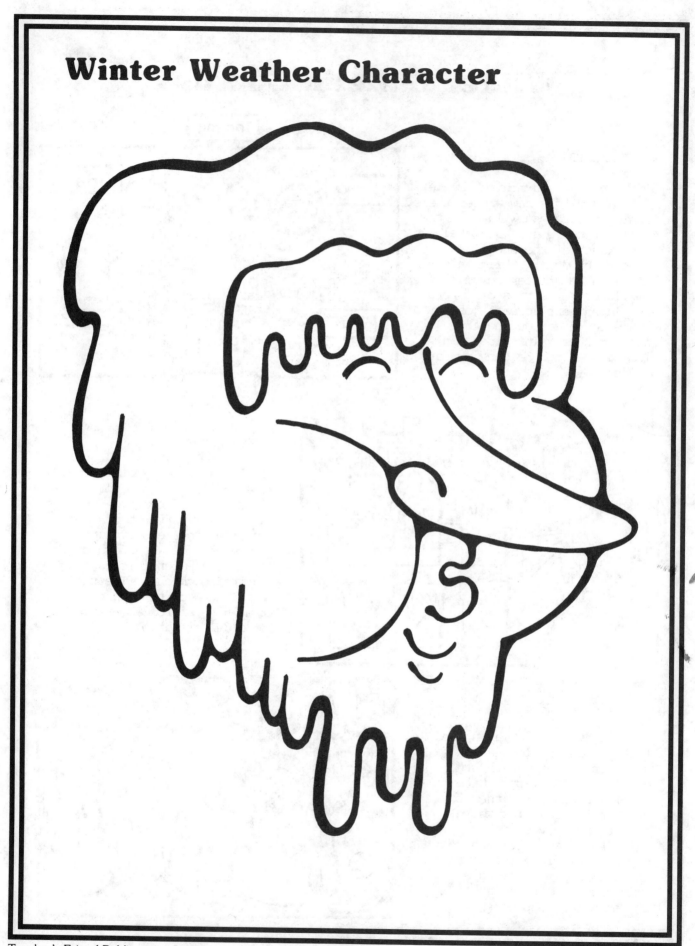

Snowflake Pattern

19

Mr. Snowman

Make Mr. Snowman from index paper. Add your own original snowman face, color, cut out and fold. Attach his hat to his left hand with a brass fastener.

20

Matching Snowman

Make several copies of snowmen and hats from colored construction paper. Use them in a variety of matching activities such as, letter recognition, math facts, opposites, words and definitions and so on.

Jack Frost

Jack Frost is an imaginary elf that supposedly creates the lacy patterns of frost on windows, trees and just about everything in the cold outdoors.

He's found in countless nursery rhymes and children's stories, often nipping people's noses with the cold. Jack Frost is often said to appear only after we have gone to sleep. He then darts from window to window painting lacy crystals of frost on each pane.

Children might like to write creative stories about Jack Frost, or descriptive poems after observing Jack's beautiful icy crystals.

Cut Jack Frost from colored paper. Color with markers or crayons. Use brass fasteners to assemble at the dots.

Teachers: You might like to award a pattern piece of Jack Frost for good behavior or completed assignments. Children can assemble the pieces together when they have collected all six.

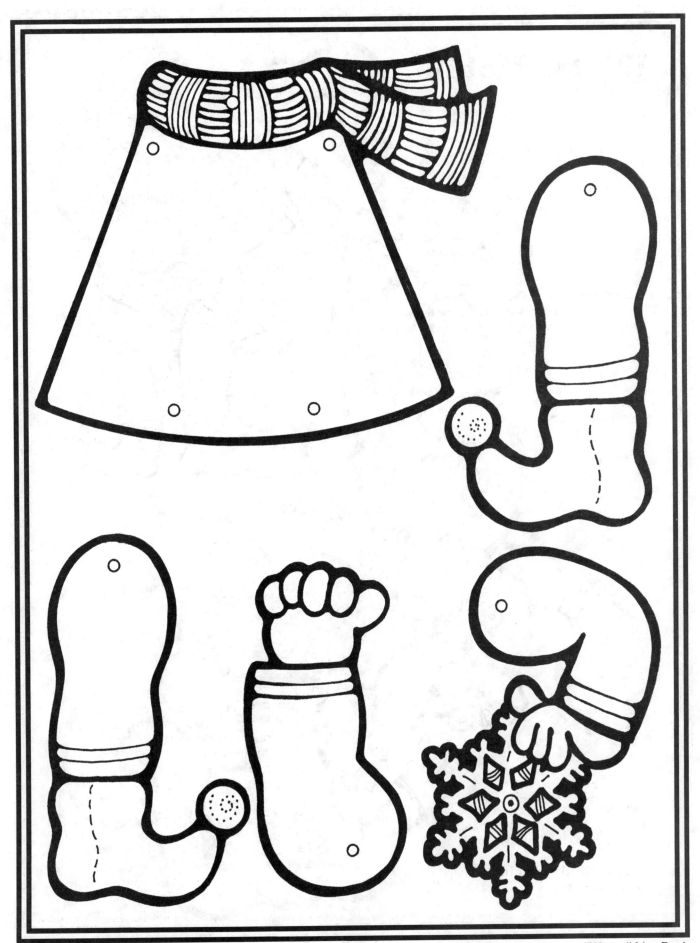

Winter Mobile

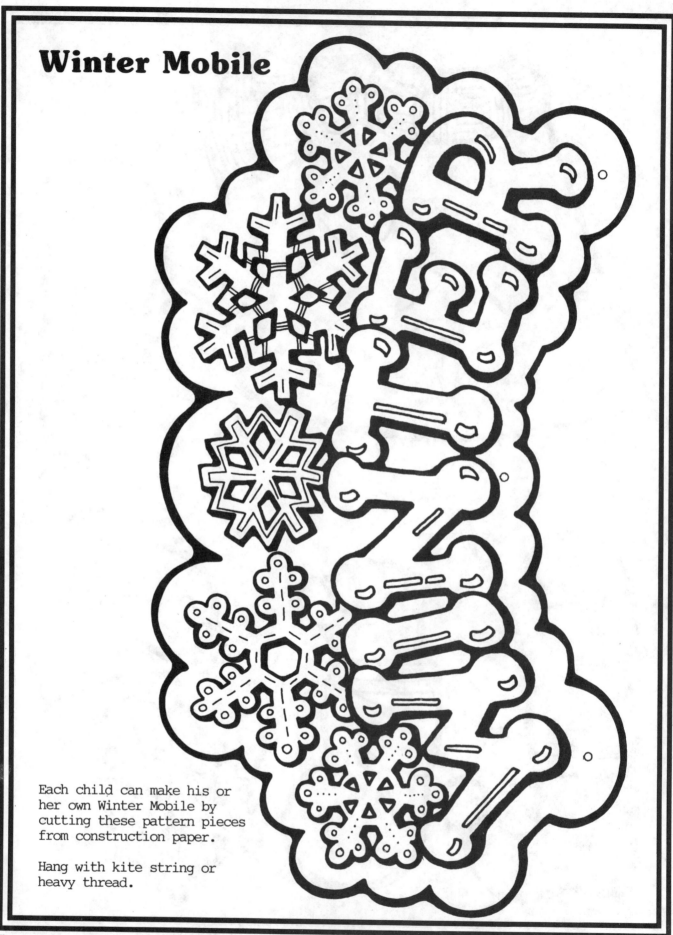

Each child can make his or her own Winter Mobile by cutting these pattern pieces from construction paper.

Hang with kite string or heavy thread.

These snowflake patterns can
also be used as bulletin
board decorations or winter
name tags.

25

Creative Writing Mittens

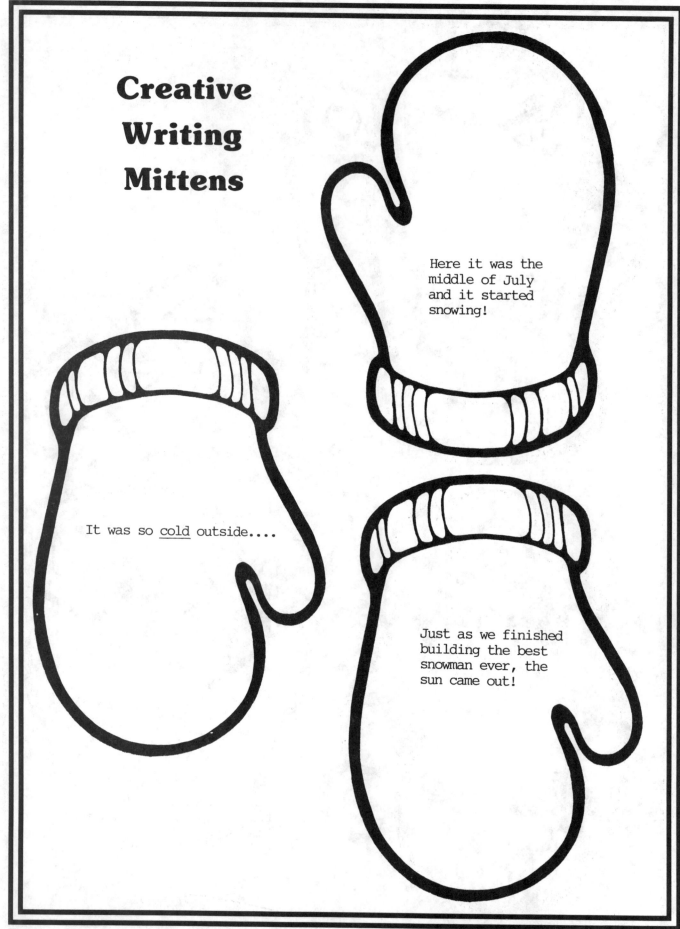

Here it was the
middle of July
and it started
snowing!

It was so <u>cold</u> outside....

Just as we finished
building the best
snowman ever, the
sun came out!

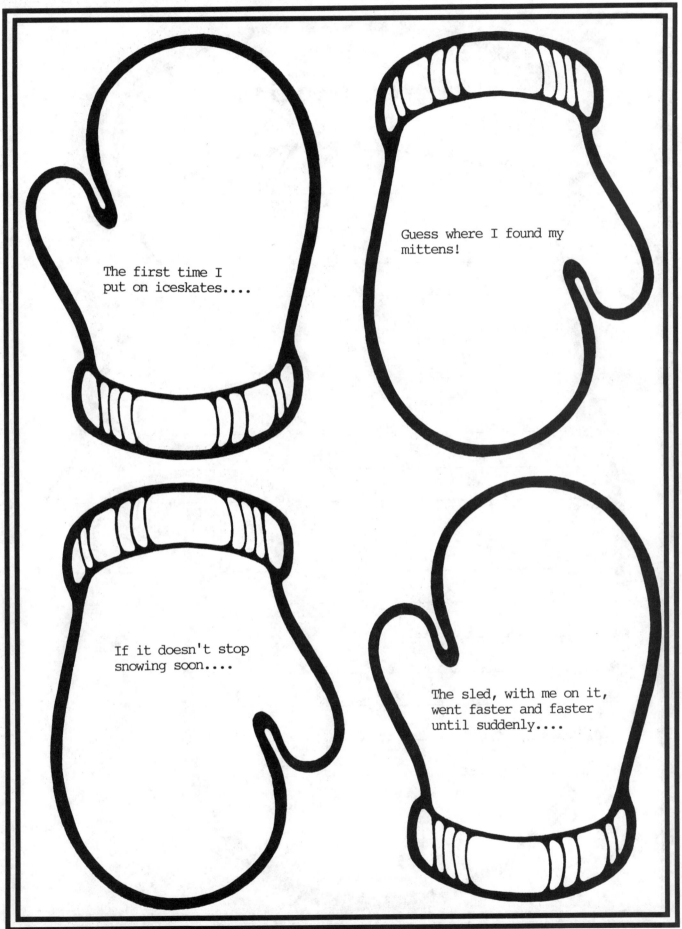

The first time I
put on iceskates....

Guess where I found my
mittens!

If it doesn't stop
snowing soon....

The sled, with me on it,
went faster and faster
until suddenly....

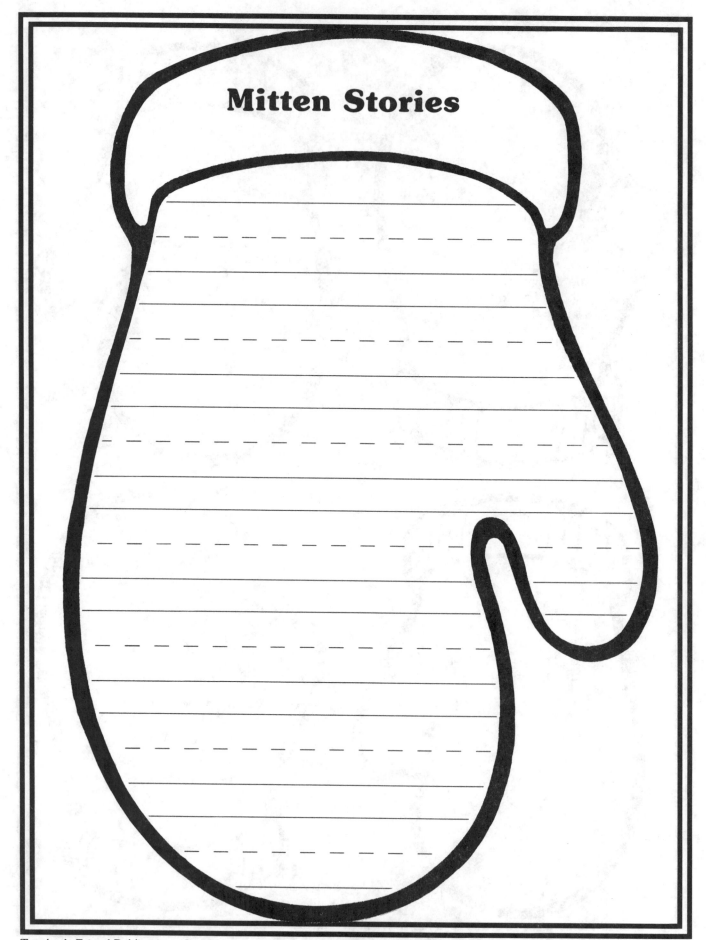

Mitten Stories

DECEMBER CLIP ART

DECEMBER AWARDS

DECEMBER ACTIVITIES

SANTA SEQUENCE CARDS

DECEMBER BULLETIN BOARDS

SANTA CHARACTER

STAND-UP SLEIGH AND REINDEER

GINGERBREAD MEN

DECEMBER FUN GLASSES

MANGER MOBILE

GIFTS FOR MOM AND DAD

MY HANUKKAH BOOK

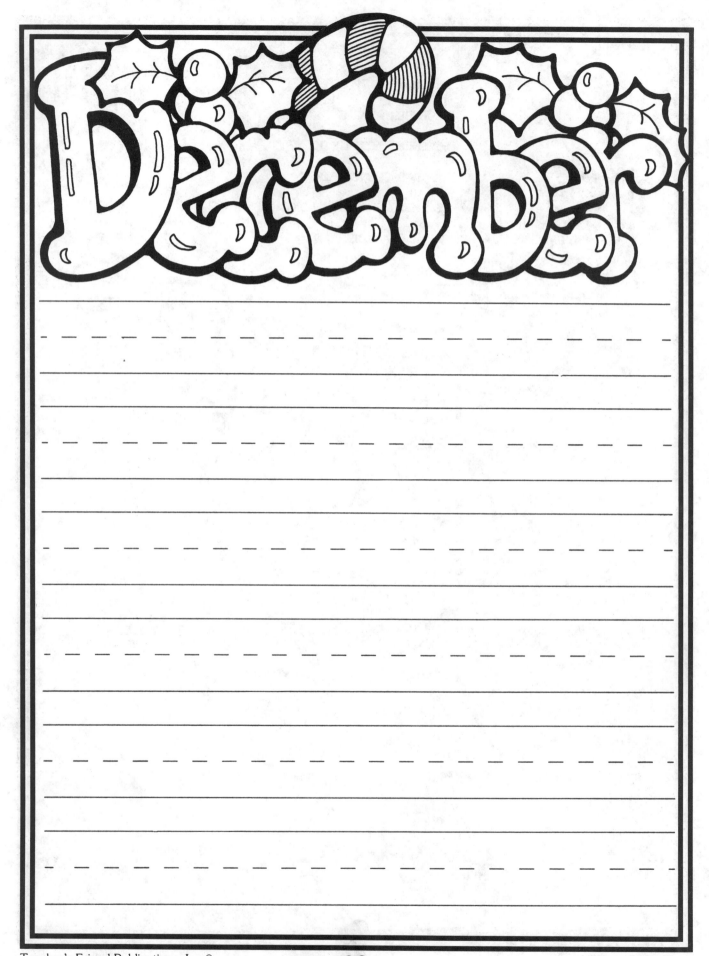

December Clip Art

Type the name of your school, address and telephone number in this space. Include your name and room number, also.

OUR DECEMBER NEWSLETTER

Suggestions for a December newsletter:

List the name of each student that was selected student of the week for the month of November.

Note the dates of Christmas vacation. Make sure that parents know which days children will not be in attendance.

Announce special holiday programs or plays being conducted by your school or in your classroom.

Tell about something special your class is currently working on.

Ask one of your students to draw several small pictures about Christmas or Hanukkah to be used in the December newsletter.

Ask your school principal to write a brief message that can be included with the December newsletter.

Ask for parent volunteers or donations for the class holiday party and/or class food drive.

Staple the December cafeteria menu to each newsletter.

Send a welcome note to a new student or a get well message to a student that has been out ill.

Suggest to parents that they encourage their children to read or catch up on incompleted school work during the holiday vacation.

Wish your students and their parents a happy holiday and wonderful new year!

SUPER STUDENT AWARD

awarded to

_____

for

_____
_____
_____

_____
Date

_____
Teacher

STUDENT OF THE MONTH

AWARDED TO

_____
Name

_____

_____

_____
Teacher

_____
Date

December Activities

DECEMBER

Winter begins when fall is done
About December twenty-one.
Our family sings with happy voices
Christmas songs; the world rejoices.
Christmas means a holly wreath
And Christmas tree with gifts beneath.
One week later is New Year's Eve.
Old Father Time is sure to leave.
At the stroke of twelve, you will hear
People shouting, "Happy New Year!"

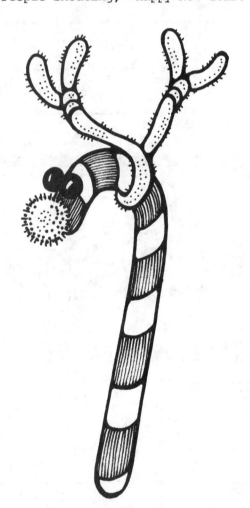

'TWAS THE NIGHT BEFORE CHRISTMAS,...

Do you need a simple classroom skit for the holidays? Try this easy but fun idea.

Assign one set of lines from the poem "A Visit From St. Nicholas" by Clement Moore, to each of your students. Ask them to illustrate their section of the poem on a large sheet of construction paper. They should also memorize their lines. On skit day, each student takes turns reciting their part of the poem and holding up their picture. Have the entire class recite the last line, "Happy Christmas to all, and to all a good night!"

Display the illustrations on the class bulletin board for a clever holiday mural.

CANDY CANE RUDOLPH

Twist two pipe cleaners around the top of a small cellophane-wrapped candy cane for Rudolph's antlers. Glue two small buttons for eyes and a red pompon for his nose. Hang Rudolph on the tree as a holiday ornament or give to a friend as a special treat.

Santa Sequence Cards

December Bulletin Boards

STOCKING STUFFERS

Your students stuff a large Christmas stocking for an easy holiday bulletin board.

Have each child write his or her name on a strip of construction paper. Ask them to cut pictures from magazines, to represent what they would like for Christmas, and glue them to the paper. Students might like to make individual stockings that can be displayed on a paper mantel.

CLASS CHOIR

Have each student draw his or her own portrait on a paper plate. Ask them to draw the mouth in a singing position. Attach a red bow to the chin of each face.

Arrange the faces on the class bulletin board, as shown, to display your class choir.

HOLIDAY DREAMS

Children can draw self portraits that are then tucked into a bulletin board quilt. (Make the quilt from old wallpaper samples.)

Place a white paper cloud above their heads and have students write or draw in their holiday dreams.

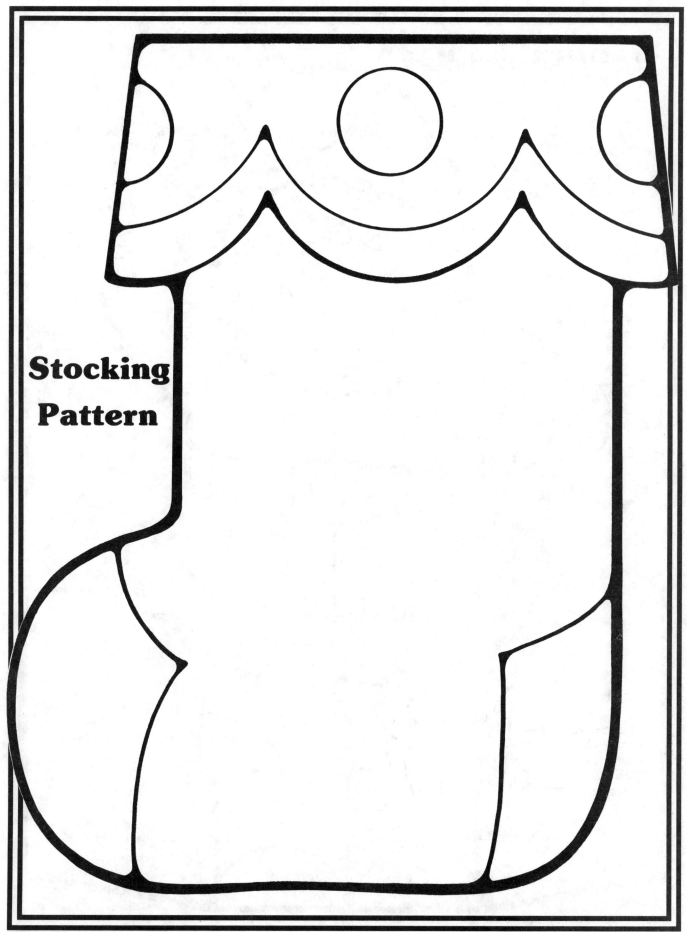

Stocking
Pattern

Santa Character

Make this Santa character from index paper. Color, cut and fold.

Stand on a table for a special Christmas decoration.

Stand-Up Reindeer

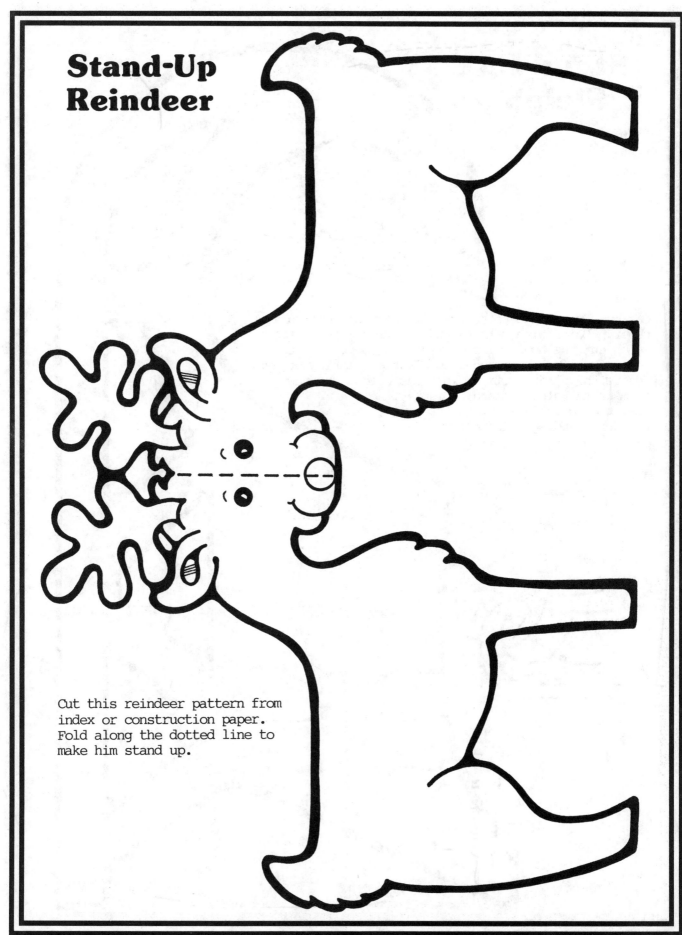

Cut this reindeer pattern from index or construction paper. Fold along the dotted line to make him stand up.

Stand-Up Sleigh

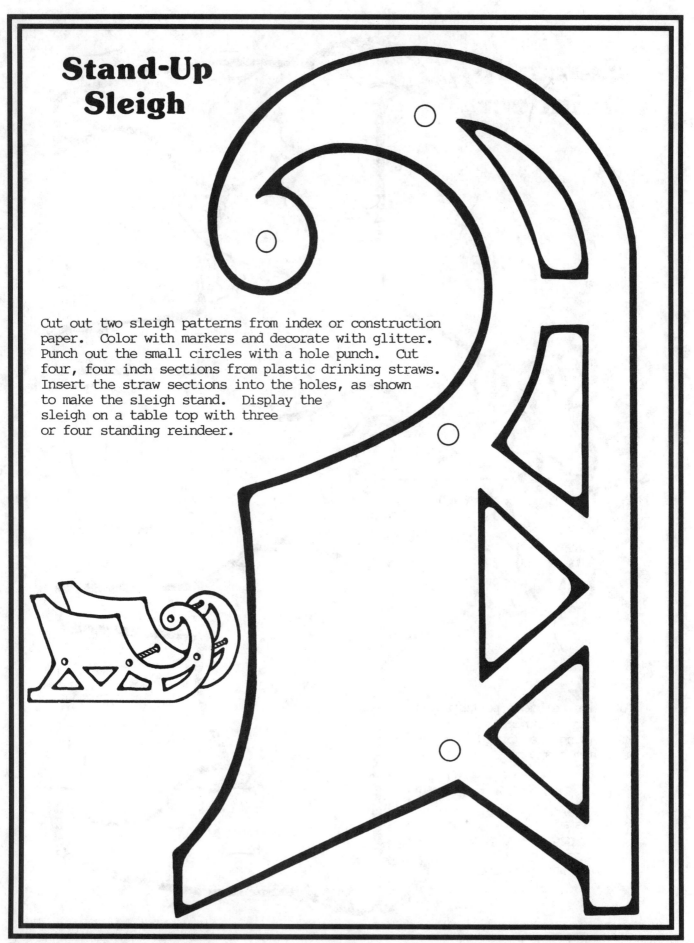

Cut out two sleigh patterns from index or construction paper. Color with markers and decorate with glitter. Punch out the small circles with a hole punch. Cut four, four inch sections from plastic drinking straws. Insert the straw sections into the holes, as shown to make the sleigh stand. Display the sleigh on a table top with three or four standing reindeer.

Stand-Up Holiday Gifts

Cut out the wreath and gifts from heavy paper. Write your own holiday message on the gifts. Fan fold along the dotted lines. Glue the wreath to the first gift and stand on a desk top for a festive decoration.

Gingerbread Men

Gingerbread men are fun to make and so good to eat!

Trace the pattern below onto cardboard and cut out. Use a package of gingerbread mix for the dough and follow directions on the box for rolled cookies. Roll the dough onto waxed paper and use the cardboard pattern to trace around, using a rounded knife. Place raisins for eyes and cinnamon red-hots for the mouth. After baking, white frosting can be applied to outline clothes and/or add buttons.

Children will enjoy following directions and helping with clean up when the reward is a freshly baked gingerbread cookie!

GINGERBREAD MEN ORNAMENTS

Make these simple paper gingerbread men ornaments from brown construction paper or heavy grocery bags. Trace the pattern and cut out. Decorate with white poster paint. Add a dash of powdered cinnamon or ginger, applied with a small amount of glue, to your gingerbread man. This will make him smell like the real thing. Attach a thread to the top of his head and hang on the Christmas tree.

A fabric version of the same gingerbread man can be made by using two cloth cut outs. Glue or stitch the two patterns together leaving a small opening. Stuff him with a cotton ball sprinkled with spices. Add real ribbon or rickrack to decorate.

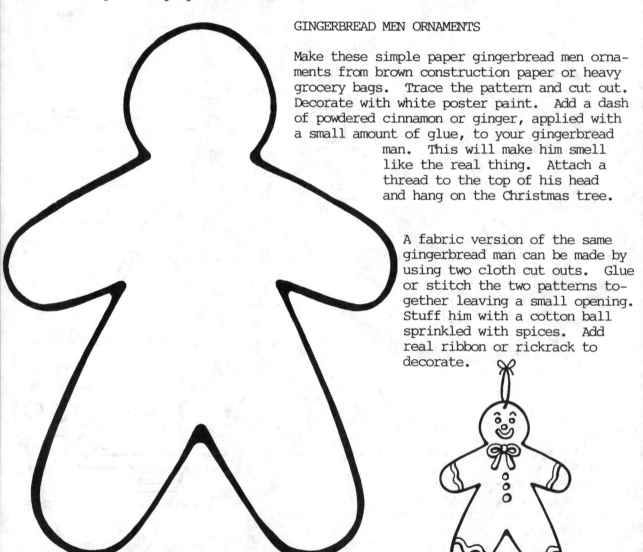

Gingerbread House Card

Copy this Gingerbread House pattern onto construction paper, color and cut out.

Fold the front of the card to the center and write a holiday message inside.

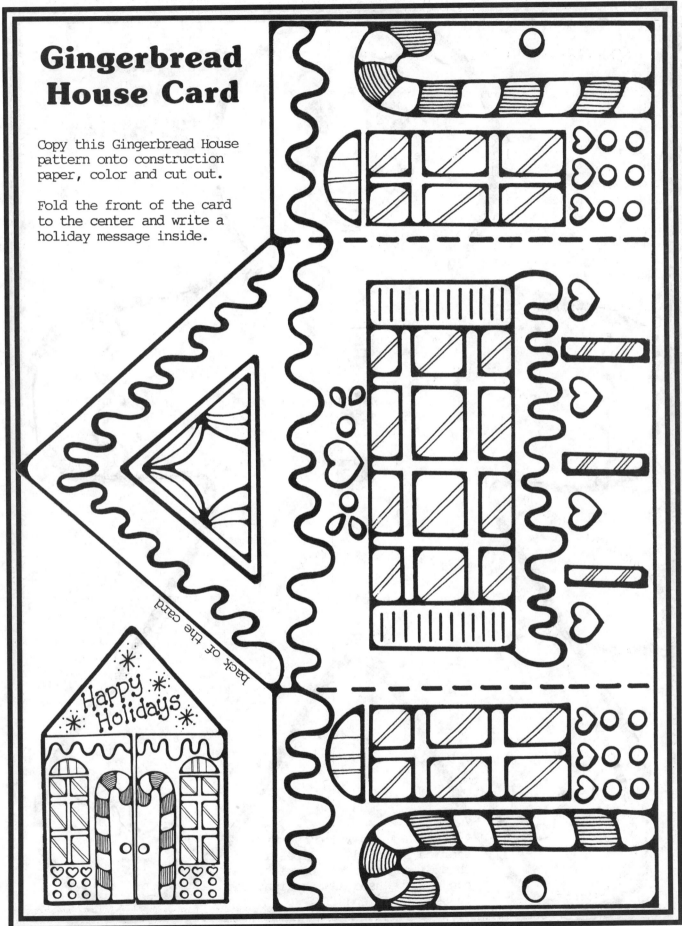

back of the card

Happy Holidays

Gingerbread Man Booklet

Ask students to write "yummy" stories or holiday recipes inside this Gingerbread Man Booklet. He can also be used as a holiday card to send to friends!

December Fun Glasses

Cut the pattern pieces from heavy
index paper and color with markers
or crayons. Attach the bows to
the frame by fitting them into the
designated slots.

HAPPY HOLIDAYS!

CUT OUT

CUT OUT

A

B

A

B

My Wish List

Holiday Writing

Manger Mobile

Each student can make his own "Manger Mobile" using these simple patterns. Cut the patterns from construction paper and assemble with thread or yarn, as shown.

Glue the angel to the top of
the manger before attaching
the string.

Handy Coin Holder

Give Dad a "handy" coin holder as a gift!

Cut two hand patterns from colored felt. Cut one or two layers of scrap fabric, slightly smaller, and place them between the two hand patterns. Stich or glue the edges of the hands together. Use small pieces of felt, yarn and sequins to add finger nails, rings, etc. to the coin holder.

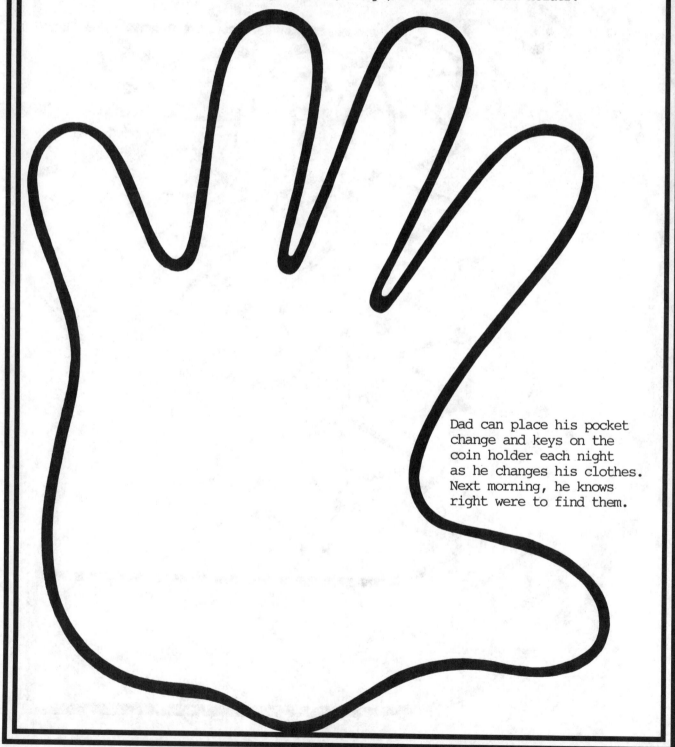

Dad can place his pocket change and keys on the coin holder each night as he changes his clothes. Next morning, he knows right were to find them.

Strawberry Potholder Gift

Mom will love this handmade potholder gift!

Cut two strawberry patterns from red felt. Cut the stem from a folded piece of green felt. A layer or two of scrap fabric, cut slightly smaller, should be placed between the two strawberry patterns. Stitch or glue the edges of the strawberry together. Glue or stitch the stem to the top, as shown. (The loop in the stem forms a convenient handle.) You might like to cross-stitch a few places on the face of the potholder as decoration.

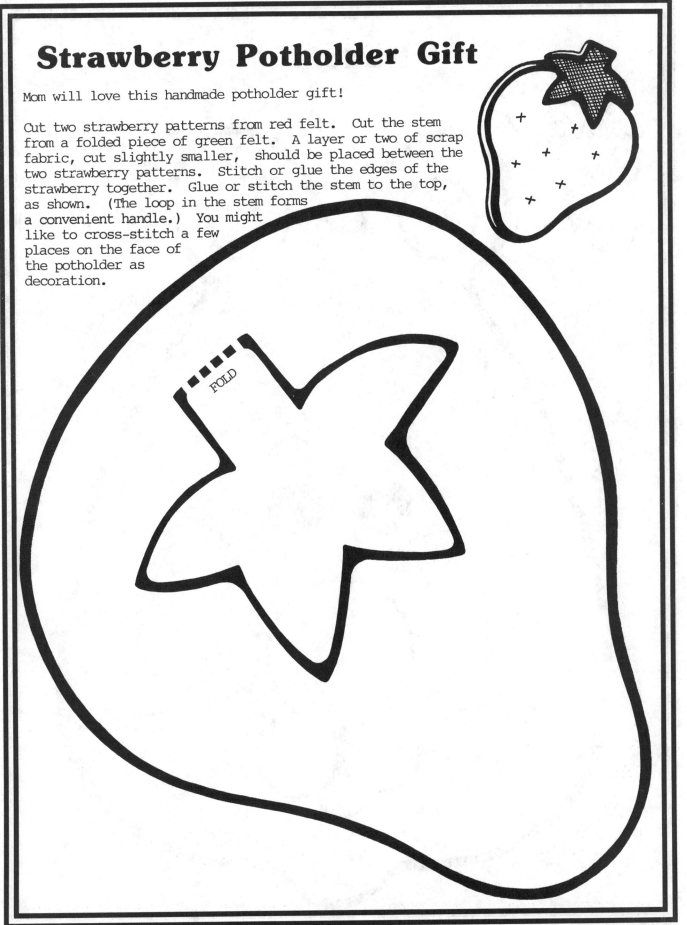

FOLD

Rudolph

Color and cut out this Rudolph pattern.

Trace both hands on brown construction paper and cut out. Glue the two hands, (or antlers) to the top of his head, as shown.

Display Rudolph on the class door or bulletin board.

My
Hanukkah
Book

HANUKKAH

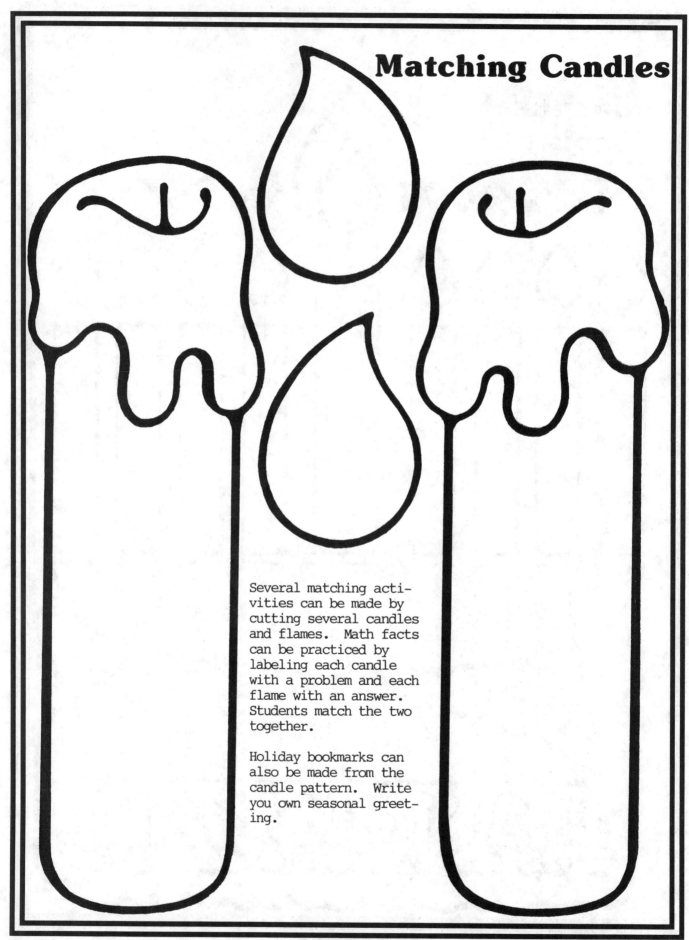

Several matching activities can be made by cutting several candles and flames. Math facts can be practiced by labeling each candle with a problem and each flame with an answer. Students match the two together.

Holiday bookmarks can also be made from the candle pattern. Write you own seasonal greeting.

JANUARY CLIP ART

JANUARY AWARDS

JANUARY ACTIVITIES

JANUARY FUN GLASSES

NEW YEAR DIARY

JANUARY BULLETIN BOARDS

TIME AWARDS

TIME CARDS

CLOCK PATTERNS

NEW YEAR'S RESOLUTION MOBILE

January Clip Art

Type the name of your school, address and telephone number in this space. Include your name and room number, also.

Suggestions for a January newsletter:

List the name of each student that was selected student of the week for the month of December.

Note the dates of Martin Luther King Day. Make sure that parents know which day or days children will not be in attendance.

Announce special programs being conducted by your school or in your classroom.

Tell about something special your class is currently working on.

Ask your school principal to write a brief message that can be included with the January newsletter.

Staple the January cafeteria menu to each newsletter.

Announce upcoming fieldtrips, class plays, spelling bees or fund raisers.

Ask one of your students to draw several small pictures about the winter season, Dr. Martin Luther King, Jr. or Chinese New Year to be used in the January newsletter.

Send a welcome note to a new student or a get well message to a student that has been out ill.

Wish each of your students and their parents a happy and successful new year!

SUPER STUDENT AWARD

awarded to

_____

for

_____
_____
_____

_____
Date

_____
Teacher

January

STUDENT OF THE MONTH

AWARDED TO

_____
Name

_____
_____

_____
Teacher

_____
Date

January Activities

JANUARY

My new calendar is temporary.
Of course it begins in January,
But when 365 days are done,
I know I'll need another one.

In January, cold weather stays
Every one of 31 days.
Football fans will watch and freeze.
But most stay home with their TV's.

RESOLUTION T-SHIRTS

Students love to make statements
with the clothes they wear. In
this case, have that statement be
a positive New Year's resolution!

Have each student bring to school a
plain colored or white T-shirt.
Students can depict their own per-
sonal resolution using permanent
colored markers. (Place a piece
of cardboard inside the T-shirt to
stop the color from bleeding through.)
You might like to display the shirts
on a class clothesline prior to let-
ting the students wear them.

To avoid the cost of real T-shirts,
simply make paper T-shirts cut from
white construction paper. These,
also, will make a great classroom
display.

TIME MARCHES ON

January offers the perfect opportunity
to teach the concept of time. You might
want to display a large clock face on
the class bulletin board, or have each
student make their own large clock face
with movable hands. The teacher can
call out a specific time and each pupil
can arrange the clock hands on his or
her clock accordingly.

With younger students, explore the concepts of past, present, future, before
and after.

JANUS

In ancient times, the Romans had a god
who was responsible for watching the
old year go and the new year come. To
do this, he had two faces so that he
could look both ways at the same time.
The Romans called this two-faced god,
Janus. Our first month, January, is
named after him.

Students might like to discuss what the
term "two-faced" means today. They may
also enjoy researching other Roman and
Greek gods and their legends.

My New Year's Resolutions

Think about the positive things
you could do to improve the
world around you. Write your
ideas in the spaces provided.

My Home _____

_____

My Classroom _____

_____

My School _____

_____

My Community _____

_____

The World _____

_____

This year, I would like to.... _____

_____

_____

If I could change one thing, it would be.... _____

_____

_____

_____

_____

January Fun Glasses

Cut the pattern pieces from heavy index paper and color with markers or crayons. Attach the bows to the frame by fitting them into the designated slots.

My Diary For

January Bulletin Boards

RING IN A NEW YOU!

Ask students to write their New Year resolutions or self improvement goals on the bell pattern. These goals might include behaviors that could be accomplished at school, such as; completion of all homework assignments for the next two weeks or receive a "B" or better on the next spelling test. Children could earn stickers when the goals are reached.

MESSAGE MYSTERY

On a large sheet of colored butcher paper, write a mystery message in large, bold letters. Cut the paper into numerous squares and make sure each student has their own piece.

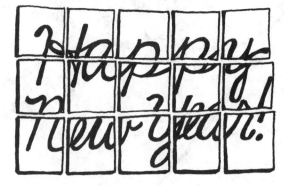

Ask the students to arrange their pieces on the class bulletin board to solve the mystery. You can use this idea anytime during the year. Students will love it!

MAKE A WISH!

Children can make their wishes known on these cute wishing wells. Ask them to write three wishes for the coming year. These might include their wish for peace on earth or a solution to the drug problem. Large Lincoln pennies can also be part of the display. (See page 99.)

name

My New Year's Resolutions

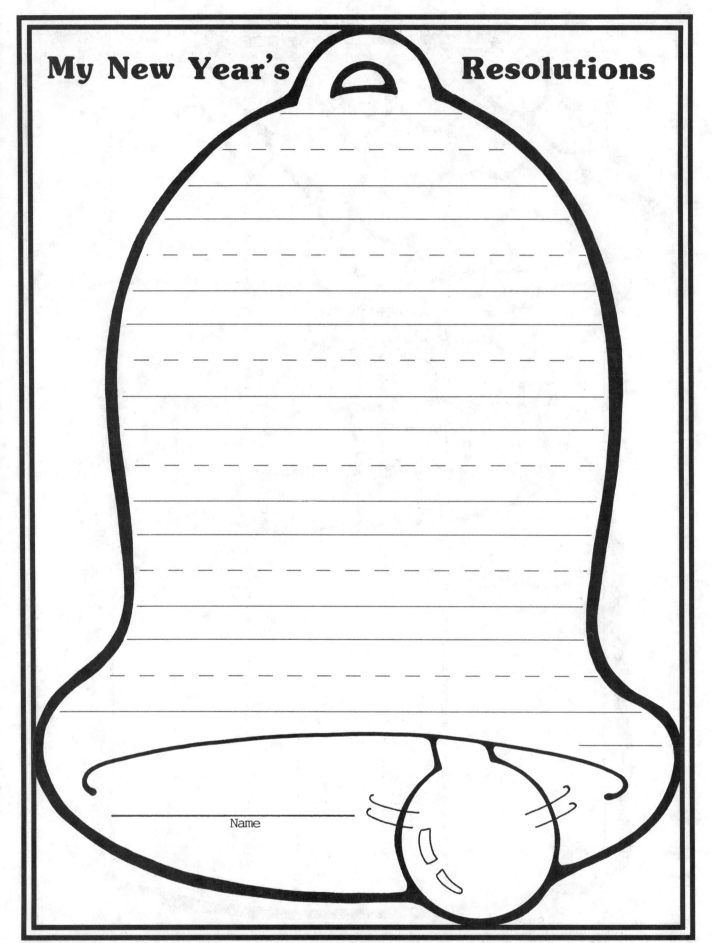

_____ Name

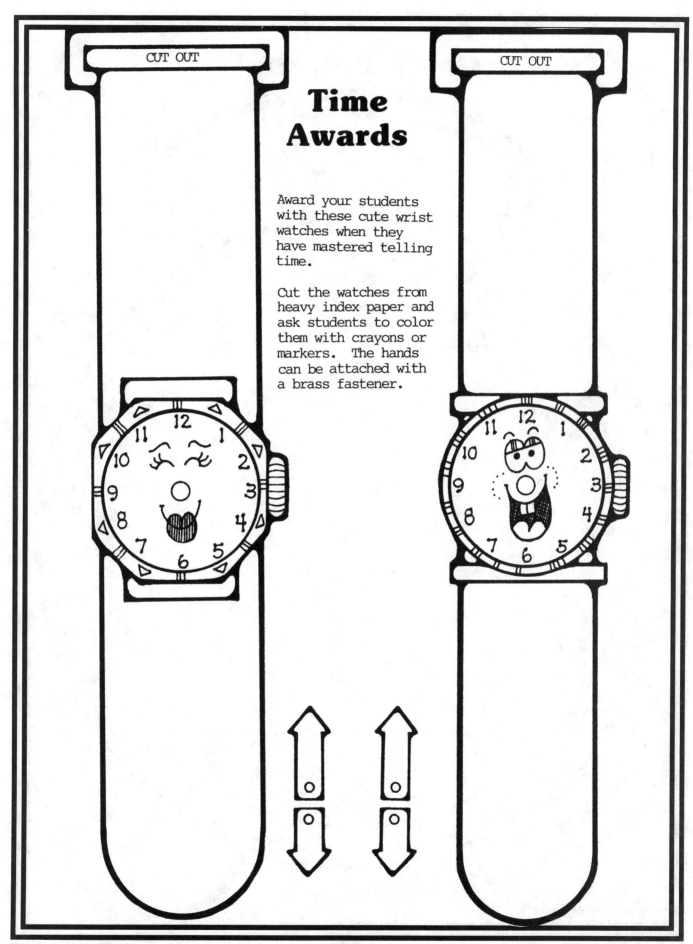

Time Awards

Award your students with these cute wrist watches when they have mastered telling time.

Cut the watches from heavy index paper and ask students to color them with crayons or markers. The hands can be attached with a brass fastener.

Clock Pattern

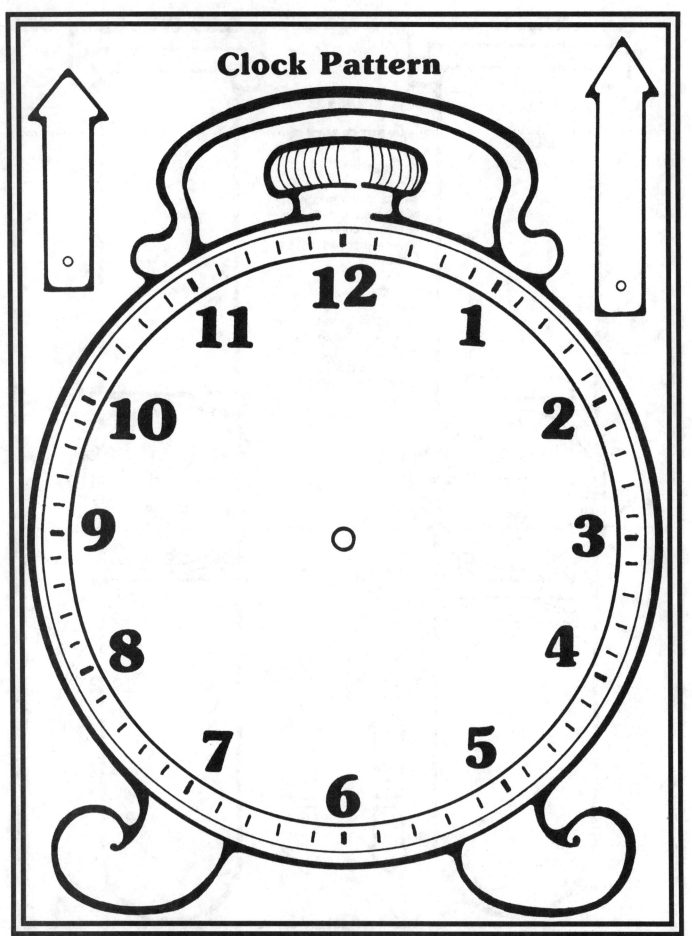

Reinforce the concepts of time by using these blank clock faces. Make several copies and draw in your own clock hands. Children can match each clock with the correct time cards, located on the next pages.

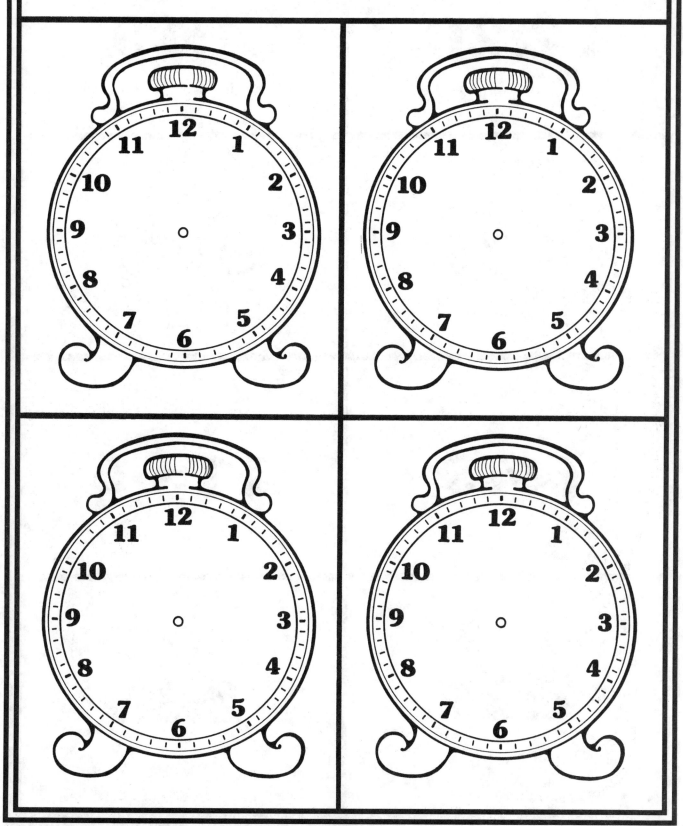

12:20	**4:15**
7:35	**3:50**
6:45	**11:05**
1:25	**2:30**

5:10	**3:15**
12:45	**7:20**
1:40	**9:30**
8:40	**6:55**

New Year's Resolution Mobile

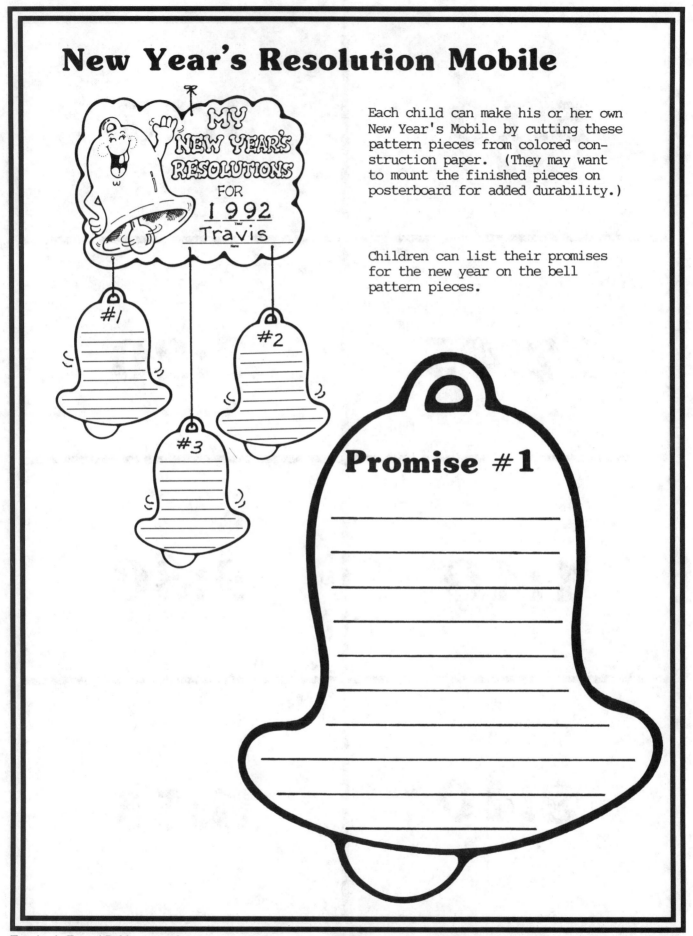

Each child can make his or her own New Year's Mobile by cutting these pattern pieces from colored construction paper. (They may want to mount the finished pieces on posterboard for added durability.)

Children can list their promises for the new year on the bell pattern pieces.

MY NEW YEAR'S RESOLUTIONS
FOR
1 9 9 2
Travis

#1

#2

#3

Promise #1

February
Clip Art

Type the name of your school, address and telephone number in this space. Include your name and room number, also.

Suggestions for a February newsletter:

List the name of each student that was selected student of the week for the month of January.

Note the dates of Washington's and Lincoln's birthdays. Make sure that parents know which days children will not be in attendance.

Announce special programs or parties being conducted by your school or in your classroom.

Ask for parent volunteers or donations for the class Valentine's Day party.

Ask one of your students to draw several small pictures about Valentine's Day or Washington's or Lincoln's birthday to be used in the February newsletter.

Ask your school principal to write a brief message that can be included with the February newsletter.

Staple the February cafeteria menu to each newsletter.

Send a welcome note to a new student or a get well message to a student that has been out ill.

This month starts a new semester in the school year. List your classroom goals, once again, for your student's parents. If your school schedules parent conferences during this month, remind them of these dates.

Announce upcoming fieldtrips, class plays, spelling bees or fund raisers.

SUPER STUDENT AWARD

awarded to

_____

for

_____

_____

_____

_____
Date

_____
Teacher

STUDENT OF THE MONTH

AWARDED TO

_____
Name

_____

_____

_____   _____
Teacher   Date

February Activities

FEBRUARY'S EXTRA DAY

Every four years as planets rotate,
Our calendar needs another date.
Add one to February—that's fine,
So February has twenty-nine.
Leap Year Day then appears
Only once every four years.
And on this day in February
A girl may ask a boy to marry.
All other days, I suppose,
Boys are encouraged to propose.

FAMOUS NAMES

Everything from states and cities
to streets and schools have been
named for George Washington and
Abraham Lincoln. Ask students to
list as many places and things
as they can named after the two
presidents. Make sure that they
consider local as well as national
and international places. Ask
them to find these places on the
classroom map.

LINCOLN AND WASHINGTON

Washington and Lincoln, as well as
many other famous Americans, appear
on our country's coins, bills and
postage stamps. Ask students to
find out the history of the Lincoln
penny and the Washington dollar bill.

ABE'S LEGS

Abe Lincoln always had long legs,
A very tall man was he.
Someone asked him how long he thought
A man's legs ought to be.

He answered quick
With look profound,
"Long enough,
To reach the ground!"

February Bulletin Boards

LINCOLN AND WASHINGTON

Display a large dollar bill and a Lincoln penny on the class bulletin board. Have students list various facts about both presidents or give them historical math problems that can be listed on the board, such as; If Washington were alive today, how old would he be? Or, How many years did the Civil War last?

VALENTINE WISHES
Using pink and red construction paper, have each student cut two heart shapes. Ask them to write their name on one heart and his or her valentine wish for the world on the other. Arrange the hearts in a giant heart shape on the class bulletin board.

BLACK HISTORY MONTH

Create an extra large matching activity using the names of famous black Americans and their individual contributions to our country. Children can use pieces of yarn to connect the name with the correct accomplishment.

Stand-Up Valentines

Be Mine | Say Yes | Kiss Me! | I Love You

Cut out all of these hearts from heavy paper. Write your own valentine messages on the smaller hearts. Fan fold along the dotted lines. Glue the larger valentine to the first heart and stand on a desk top for a Valentine's Day decoration.

February Fun Glasses

Cut the pattern pieces from heavy index paper and color with markers or crayons. Attach the bows to the frame by fitting them into the designated slots.

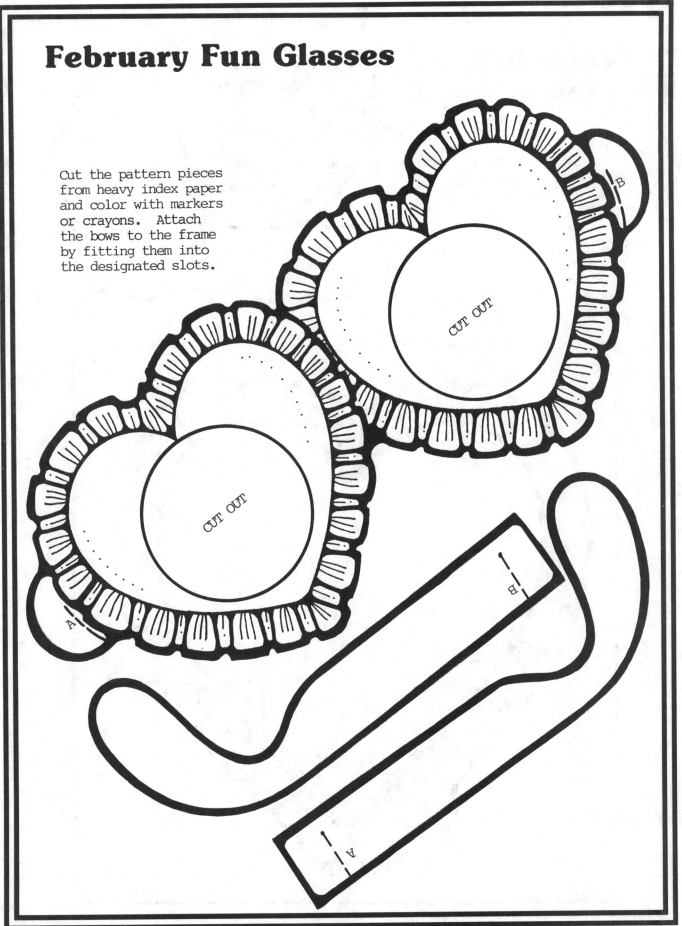

Valentine Frame

This simple Valentine Frame makes a wonderful February craft or a great gift for mom or dad.

Copy the pattern to a piece of folded index or construction paper. Cut out the inside of the heart shape and glue a child's photo inside the folded pieces. A simple stand can be made by stapling the discarded heart to the back of the frame, as shown.

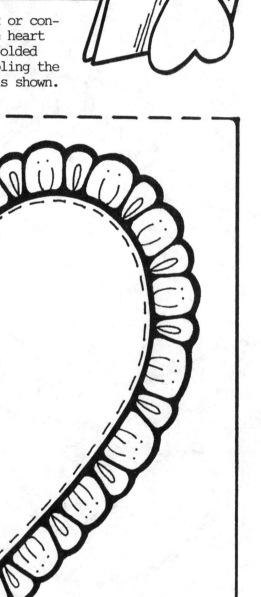

CUT OUT

Woven Valentines

This woven valentine is easily made by cutting two patterns, one from red paper and one from white. The pattern is folded in half and cut up the center in three places.

Hold one pattern in each hand. Carefully weave the first loop of the piece in your right hand, under and over the piece in your left hand. Weave each of the loops in the same way.

When completed, it will look like a checkerboard, as shown. Staple a handle to the top of the valentine and fill with hard candy.

You might like to enlarge the pattern and make an extra large woven valentine. It could be used to hold all of your valentines collected on February 14th.

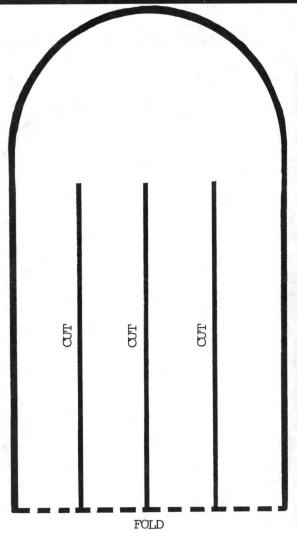

CUT   CUT   CUT

FOLD

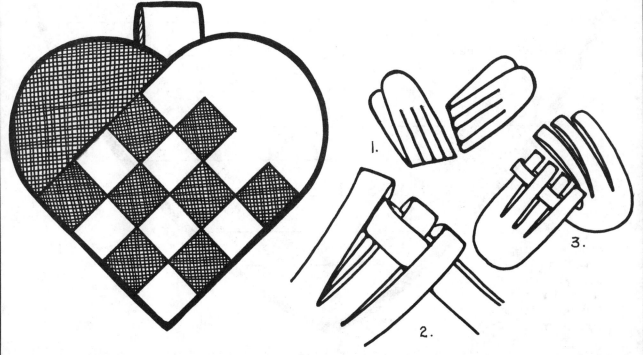

1.

2.

3.

Valentine Tales

Staple a crepe paper ruffle around your valentine after you've written your story.

Matching Heart Halves

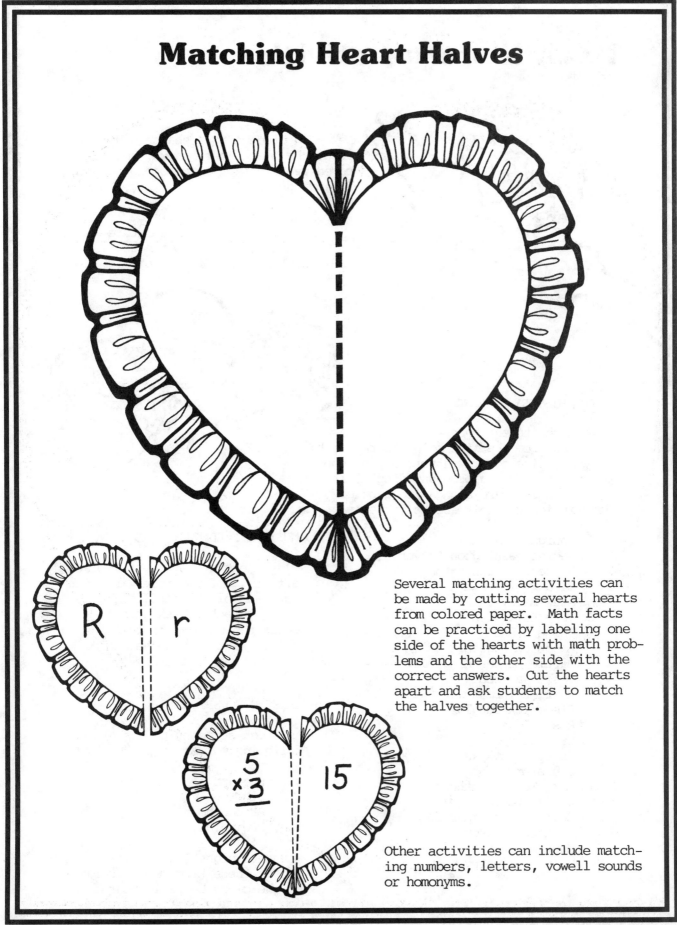

Several matching activities can be made by cutting several hearts from colored paper. Math facts can be practiced by labeling one side of the hearts with math problems and the other side with the correct answers. Cut the hearts apart and ask students to match the halves together.

Other activities can include matching numbers, letters, vowell sounds or homonyms.

Black History Activities

Ask each student to research and write about one black American who has contributed greatly in one or more of the following areas:

Education   Science
Politics   Literature
Athletics   Business
Entertainment   Medicine

BLACK HISTORY RESEARCH

Have each student choose a famous black American from the list below to research. They may like to draw a portrait of the person they have chosen and display it on the class board along with a brief description of their accomplishments.

Thurgood Marshall
George Washington Carver
Booker T. Washington
Ella Fitzgerald
Alex Haley
Duke Ellington
Jesse Owens
Langston Hughes
Martin Luther King, Jr.
Jesse Jackson
Harriet Tubman
Frederick Douglas
Rosa Parks
Hank Aaron
Crispus Attucks
Louis Armstrong
Mary McLeod Bethune
Wilma Rudolph
Charles Richard Drew
Michael Jackson
Muhammad Ali
Ralph Abernathy

MUSICAL FEELINGS

Play the music of several black artists. If possible, introduce jazz and black gospel music to your students. Ask them to write about their moods or feelings while listening to the music.

CLASS DISCUSSIONS

Ask your students to discuss the following words:

Freedom
Liberty
Brotherhood
Prejudice

Students might like to illustrate one of these terms and display it on the class bulletin board.

A Famous Black American

Contribution Patterns

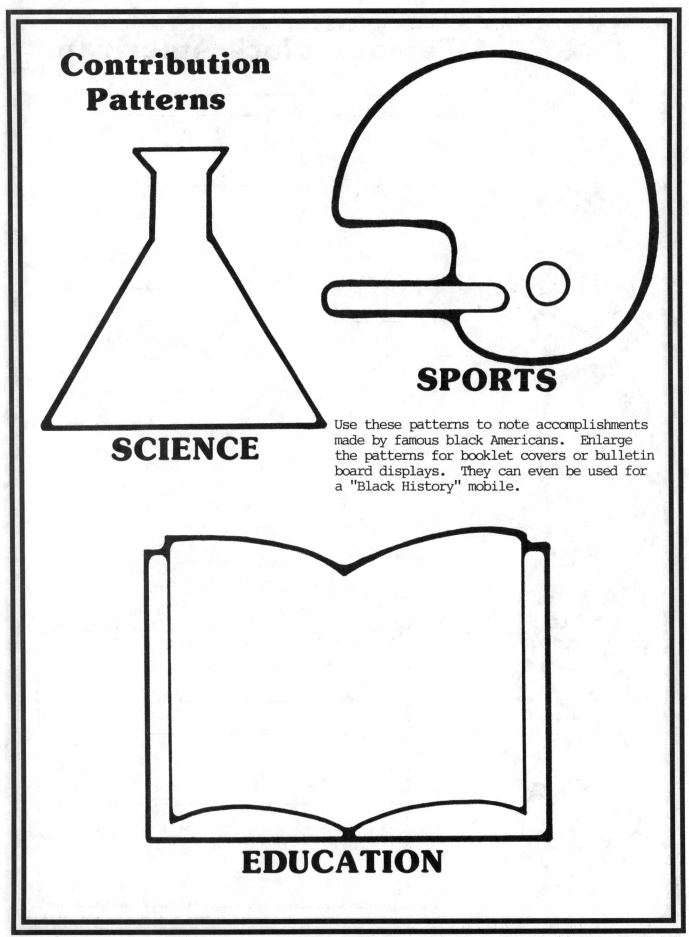

SPORTS

SCIENCE

Use these patterns to note accomplishments made by famous black Americans. Enlarge the patterns for booklet covers or bulletin board displays. They can even be used for a "Black History" mobile.

EDUCATION

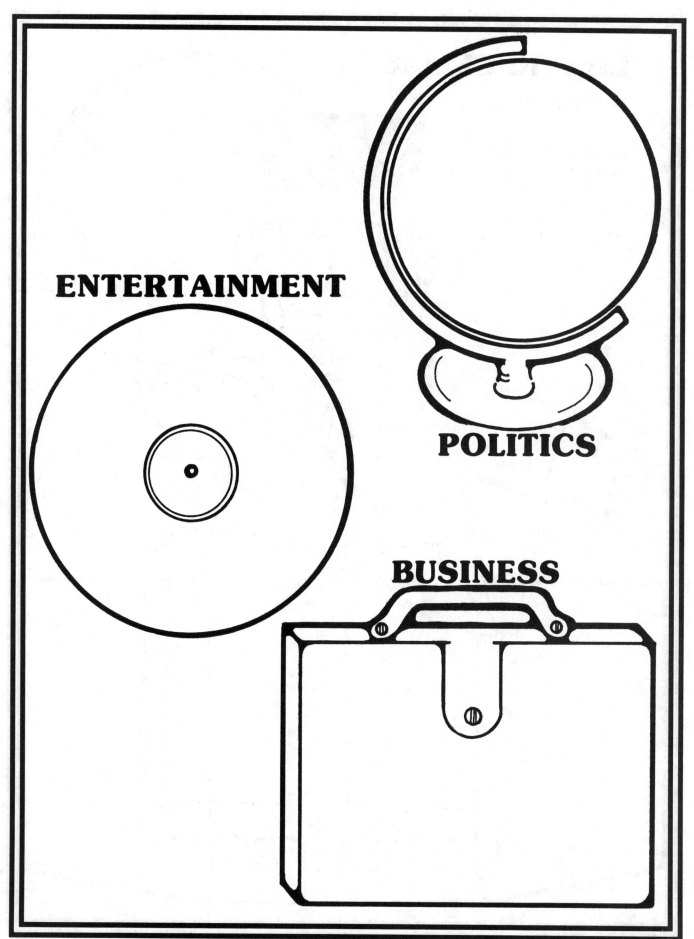

ENTERTAINMENT

POLITICS

BUSINESS

Lincoln Character

Make this Abraham Lincoln character from index or construction paper. Color, cut and fold. Attach the scroll to his right hand. Stand him on a table to celebrate the president's birthday.

Washington Character

Make this George Washington character from index paper. Color, cut and fold. Attach the hatchet to his right hand. Stand him on a table to celebrate the president's birthday.

DAY GAME

Make your own task cards for this game that two, three or four children can play.

WASHINGTON

FINISH

15. 16. 17. 18. 19. 20. 21. 22. 23. 24. 25. 26. 27. 28.

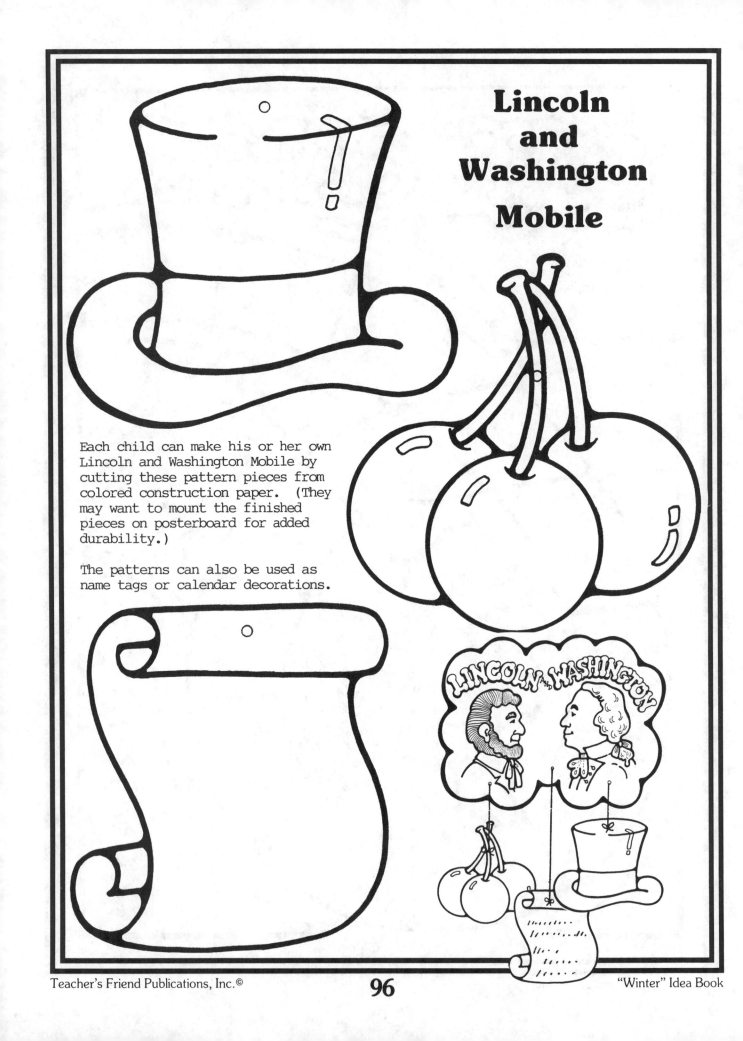

Lincoln and Washington Mobile

Each child can make his or her own Lincoln and Washington Mobile by cutting these pattern pieces from colored construction paper. (They may want to mount the finished pieces on posterboard for added durability.)

The patterns can also be used as name tags or calendar decorations.

Washington Dollar

Use this Washington dollar pattern as a booklet cover for a report on the first president.

Lincoln Penny

Use this Lincoln Penny pattern for booklet covers or bulletin board displays. Copy the pattern onto "copper" colored construction paper.

MY PRESIDENTS
REPORT

_____

BASKETBALL ACTIVITIES

BASKETBALL CHARACTER

SHOOT FOR THE HOOP GAME

CREATIVE WRITING BASKETBALLS

BASKETBALL BULLETIN BOARDS

MY BASKETBALL BOOK

Basketball Activities

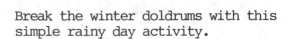

BASKETBALL HEIGHTS

You have to be especially tall
To qualify for basketball.
All players are, of course, quite strong.
Their legs and arms are extra long.
The ball is dribbled on the floor,
Thrown through the basket for a score.
I love to watch this lively sport
But, rather be playing on the court.
This game has been my great desire
If only I'd grown inches higher.
Did you ever hear of a team or sport
Just for people who are short?

RAINY DAY BASKETBALL

Break the winter doldrums with this simple rainy day activity.

Divide your class into two teams. Have each team player shoot free shots into a waste basket using a crumpled piece of paper or a light-weight foam rubber ball. Keep score and award the winning team an extra five minutes of free time.

You might want to give players a math problem to solve or a word to spell before they are permitted to shoot for a basket.

Basketball Bingo

This game offers an exciting way to introduce students to basketball vocabulary words. Give each child a copy of the bingo words listed below or write the words on the chalkboard. Ask students to write any 24 words on his or her bingo cards. Use the same directions you might use for regular bingo.

(Students might like to use some of these words in a creative writing assignment.)

BASKETBALL	FREE THROW	GUARD	COACH
COURT	CENTER	JUMP SHOT	BASKET
TEAM	FORWARD	BASKET	PENALTY
SCORE	BACK COURT	OUT OF BOUNDS	SHOT
OFFICIAL	FRONT COURT	FOUL	BENCH
REFEREE	DRIBBLING	SHOOT	NET
UMPIRE	LAYUP	SLAM DUNK	PASS
OFFENSE	HOLDING	HALFTIME	BOUNCE
DEFENSE	HOOK SHOT	HOOP	TIME CLOCK
ZONE	CHARGING	BACKBOARD	GYMNASIUM

Match the Basket and Ball

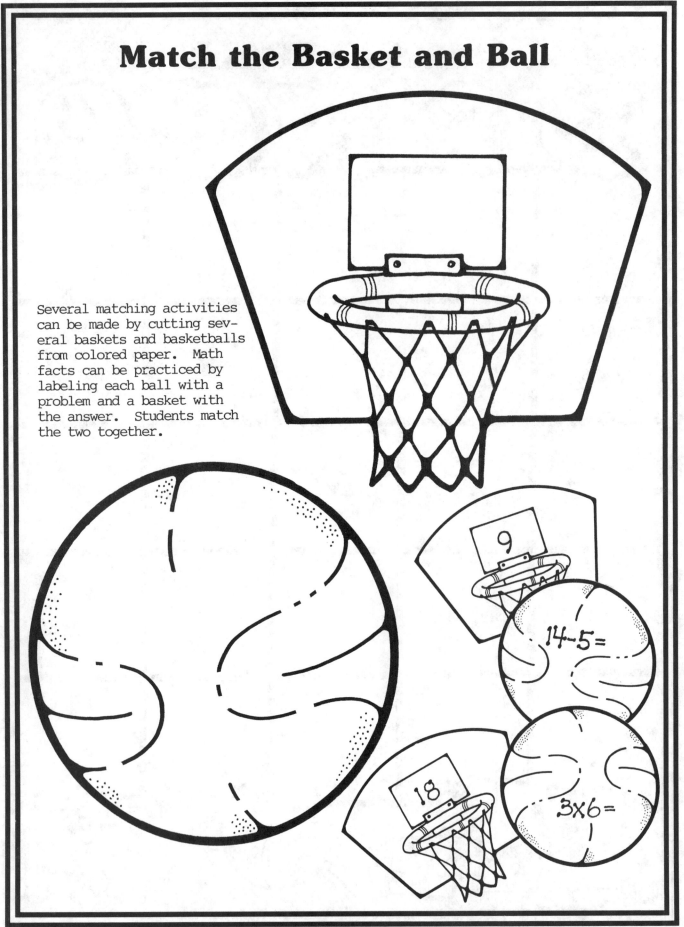

Several matching activities can be made by cutting several baskets and basketballs from colored paper. Math facts can be practiced by labeling each ball with a problem and a basket with the answer. Students match the two together.

Basketball Character

Make this Basketball Character from index paper. Color, cut and fold. Attach the basketball to his right hand.

Stand several players on a table top and pretend to play your own championship game.

START

SHOOT
FOR THE
HOOP!

TEACHERS: Two, three or four children can play this game. Make your own task cards or write math problems, that must be solved, on each basketball.

The basketball missed the hoop and landed in a most unusual place.

The entire team changed into their magic basketball shoes during halftime.

Just then the player with the ball tripped on his own shoe lace...

Creative
Writing
Basketball

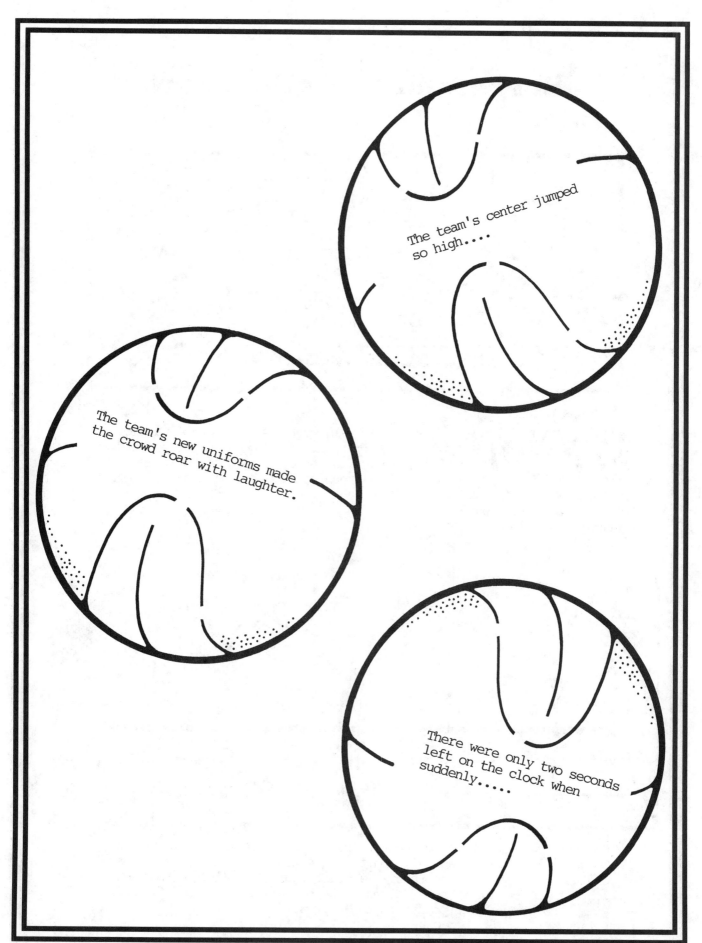

Basketball Bulletin Boards

SHOOT FOR EXCELLENCE!

Cut slits in a piece of pleated paper to create a three dimensional net for your hoop!

Display a large basket, ball and pair of hands for this motivating bulletin board. You may wish to display good work papers in and around the basketball hoop.

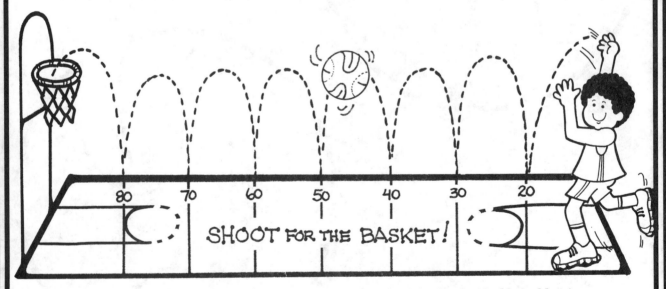

SHOOT FOR THE BASKET!

Monitor classroom goals or fund raisers with this basketball bulletin board. Display a basketball court on the board with a basket at one end and a player at the other. Mark the court to indicate the various goals to be accomplished. "Bounce" the basketball down the field as your students collect points in the contest.

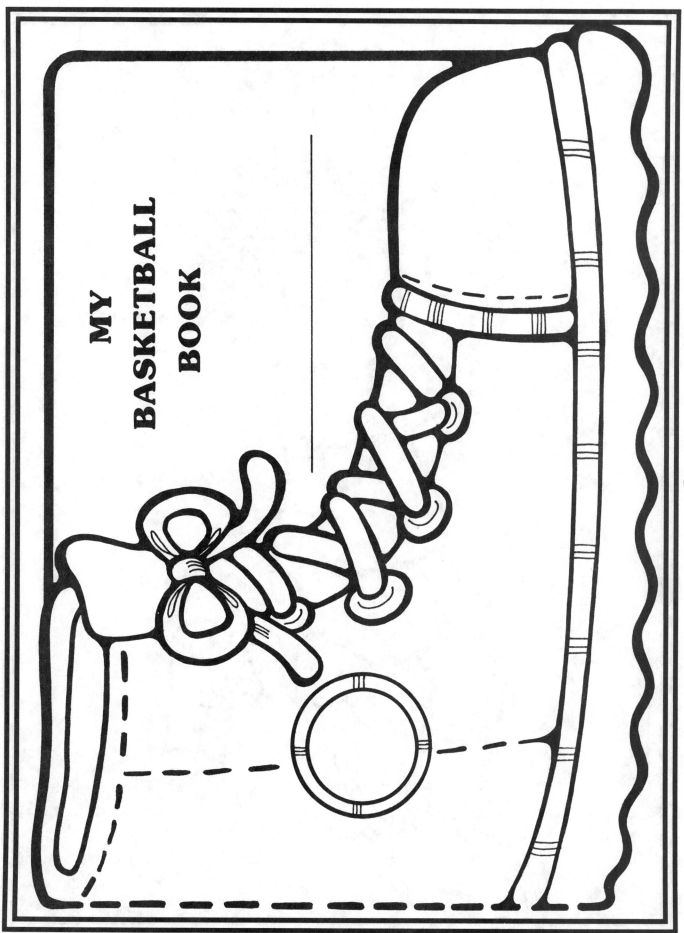

MY
BASKETBALL
BOOK